F A T H E R   P R I C E

Shortly before leaving for China

FATHER PRICE OF MARYKNOLL

A SHORT SKETCH OF THE LIFE OF

REVEREND THOMAS FREDERICK PRICE

MISSIONER IN NORTH CAROLINA
CO-FOUNDER OF MARYKNOLL
MISSIONER IN CHINA

Compiled from the letters of his friends
by a priest of Maryknoll

PUBLISHED BY THE
CATHOLIC FOREIGN MISSION SOCIETY
OF AMERICA
MARYKNOLL   :   :   :   NEW YORK

Nihil Obstat:
ARTHUR J. SCANLAN, S.T.D.
Censor of Books

Imprimatur:
✠ PATRICK J. HAYES, D.D.
Archbishop of New York

DECEMBER, 1922

Dedicated to
Blessed Bernadette Soubirous,
Child of the Immaculate Conception.

ACKNOWLEDGMENT

The compiler wishes to acknowledge with gratitude letters from

REVEREND MICHAEL A. IRWIN
Newton Grove, North Carolina

REVEREND WILLIAM F. O'BRIEN
Durham, North Carolina

REVEREND A. R. FREEMAN
Goldsboro, North Carolina

REVEREND WILLIAM B. HANNON
Asheville, North Carolina

MISS MARGARET PRICE
Wilmington, North Carolina

and others, who have supplied data for this narrative.

PREFACE

FATHER PRICE, the subject of this little book, would shrink at the idea of its publication. We who knew and loved him have felt, however, that it is good to manifest to others the light of his splendid faith and the strength of his untiring zeal. We need the spectacle of such souls as his, and only wish that more material could have been gathered and more of the words that fell from his priestly lips preserved.

— JAMES A. WALSH
Superior of Maryknoll

CONTENTS

ILLUSTRATIONS

FOREWORD

From "The Catholic Transcript," Hartford, Connecticut:

" Not since the passing of St. Francis Xavier has an event of more striking import to the Christian Church taken place in the Far East, than that which occurred there recently in the death of Reverend Thomas F. Price, of the American Foreign Missions.

" Other missioners, some of whom won the martyr's crown, have died at their posts in the Orient, but they were representative of older missionary movements, and their deaths, however heroic, were only incidents and episodes in the long history of an established order. Father Price was a pioneer and a harbinger of new and great things to come.

" The work and the movement which he represented is in its infancy, but it is already big and mighty with promise. ' The blood of martyrs is the seed of the Church ': antiquity has sent us this message — a message

xiii

which carries us back to the days of persecution, when heroes rushed to death in support of the doctrines which they were sent to proclaim. It is a true and inspiring saying, one of the sacred heritages of the Christian Church.

" If the blood of the martyrs is fecund, why not the labors, the anxious vigils, the sacrifices, and the moral heroism of those who leave all to go forth to proclaim the gospel of the Crucified? Are not all these things, and the hidden things of the apostle's spirit, a source of divine fecundity? It must be so, for with God, and before His tribunal, nothing is lost, and ' to those who love God all things work together for good.'

" As the ashes of this devoted apostle become compounded with the dust of China, the missioners of Maryknoll will feel that they have a special claim to the soil of the Orient. The seeds of a new apostolate are planted there — the seed from which an abundant soul-harvest is to follow.

" The story of the life of this apostle is briefly told. It was a life wholly spent in the conquest of souls. He was a good man, absolutely devoted to the regeneration of his fellows, a man of mortification and of high and serene converse with Heaven, one of the most austere and self-effacing priests that have ever illustrated the clerical body of the United States. If there is a crown for heroic sacrifice, and if the voice of the apostle has a peculiar potency, Maryknoll has an irresistible intercessor before the Throne of Grace."

I

EARLY DAYS

FATHER PRICE
OF MARYKNOLL

I

EARLY DAYS

REVEREND THOMAS FREDER–
ICK PRICE, the fifth son of Alfred
Lanier Price and Clarissa Bond Price, was
born on August 19, 1860. Most of his an-
cestors were among the early English immi-
grants who settled in North Carolina, but
there was also a trace of Irish blood in the
family, from an ancestor named Brady.
The Bonds and the Prices are well-respected
families living in the eastern part of the
state, the home of the family on the ma-
ternal side being near Bath, the oldest town
in North Carolina. One member of this
family was an officer in the Revolution.

Mr. Alfred Lanier Price was editor for
a time of a newspaper in Washington, District of Columbia. Later he became well-

known as the able editor of the *Wilmington Daily Journal,* the first daily paper in the state, published in Wilmington, North Carolina, from 1848 to 1872. Mr. Price, like all the other members of the Price family, was an Episcopalian, but shortly before his death, moved by the good example of his devout wife and his children, he embraced the true Faith.

Miss Clara Bond was converted from Methodism when eighteen years of age. For a long time she had been attracted to the Catholic Faith but had found our devotion to the Blessed Virgin a real stumbling block to her acceptance. God took pity on her honest fears and gave her the grace, not only of belief, but also of most devoted love for our Holy Mother, — a love that she in turn kindled in the hearts of her children and that found its most ardent expression in the life of Father Price. Because of her conversion, Miss Bond was compelled to leave home, her father disinheriting her. She was also prevented by the same indignant parent from

*ALFRED LANIER PRICE, FATHER OF
FATHER PRICE*

entering a convent in Charleston, where she wished to prepare for the religious life. It seems to have been God's design that she should enter the married state instead, for three of her children consecrated themselves to God, her two oldest daughters becoming nuns and one son a priest.

Sent away from her father's house, Miss Bond moved to Washington, a thriving town on the Pamlico River a few miles above her mother's home, and there took up her residence with Doctor Gallagher's family. Doctor Gallagher had come from Philadelphia and his was one of the two or three devout Catholic families then living in Washington. It was in this city that Miss Bond met and later married Mr. Price. Shortly after their marriage they moved to Wilmington, which became their permanent residence.

God blessed the couple with ten children, five boys and five girls. The two oldest daughters became religious in the community of Our Lady of Mercy, founded by

5

Bishop England, the first Bishop of Charleston. One of the religious, Sister Mary Catherine, is still living at the mother-house in Belmont; the other, Sister Agnes, died while young. Sister Catherine is one of the oldest members of the community, but she is still noted for her zeal and her great willingness to work for God's poor.

In gratitude for his hospitality when she sorely needed it, and mindful of the impressions she had received from the edifying lives of Doctor Thomas Frederick Gallagher and his devoted wife, Mrs. Price wished one of her children to be named after him. Accordingly the name of Thomas Frederick was given to Father Price, in memory of the conscientious physician who preached the Faith by living the life of a practical apostle in the midst of thousands of our separated brethren, when the open profession of the Catholic Faith by a gentleman in a public position meant not only the loss of much desirable patronage, but also social ostracism.

6

Mrs. Price is remembered in Wilmington as a very modest, devout, and charitable woman. The venerable Monsignor Mackin, of Washington, bears witness to this statement, for on one occasion when, as a young lad, he entered a Catholic church in Wilmington and knelt before the Blessed Sacrament in prayer and adoration, he was very much edified by the deep reverence and gracious modesty of a lady who was fixing the altar. He afterwards learned that this was Mrs. Price. By those who knew her, she was regarded as a saint. She spent much time in prayer, and all the rest of it in good works. She asked God to give her children trials to perfect them, to let them have their purgatory on this earth, and to take them out of life if they should be in danger of losing their souls, — if such were His Holy Will.

In the ages of faith, good Catholic mothers prayed and promised God that, if He blessed them with offspring, and their offspring were acceptable to Him, they would only too gladly consecrate them to His service. So Mrs. Price prayed, and no doubt the prayers and sacrifices of this saintly mother obtained from God the priceless vocation vouchsafed to her son. Thomas Frederick Price never forgot the early training he received from his mother. The seed of piety that she planted gave forth an early shoot and its growth was ever fostered by the serious, prayerful lad. Father Mark Gross, whose litany of good works and charities to God's poor is still said by the tried and faithful Catholics scattered over the Carolina missions, one day asked young Thomas Frederick if he intended studying for the priesthood.

" Yes, Father," was the immediate reply.

" Then, Thomas," said the holy and zealous missioner, " you should begin saying daily five *Our Fathers* and five *Hail Marys* to become a good priest."

To this young Thomas — more often called by his second name — replied, in the innocence that bespoke the mother's whole-

8

some influence on the heart of her son, " Father, I have done that for a long time."

Father Price, when a boy, was a quiet little fellow. His sister Mary says: " Sometimes I can still see dear little Freddie, with his little white head and his sweet little face; quiet and unobtrusive in his manner, obedient and polite. When at home, he was always reading." And it seems that youthful Fred's favorite attitude while reading was " on his back."

He never attended secular schools, but began at a little Catholic school taught by his two older sisters, Mary and Margaret, who later became Sisters Catherine and Agnes of the Mercy Convent. After his sisters gave up their school, Frederick attended a boys' school taught by the priests in the basement of the church. When he was about fifteen years of age, he resolved to go to Baltimore to be educated for the priesthood.

It is of faith, that God's providential care is over all but it is in a special manner over those who have served Him from their youth. This providential care was early manifested in the life of young Frederick Price. On Saturday, September 16, 1876, he sailed from Wilmington, on the steamer *Rebecca Clyde*, for Baltimore. After a very stormy night, the ship was wrecked off Ocracoke Inlet, Cape Hatteras. The captain, mate, and nearly all the crew were lost. Frederick Price, with some others, clung to the wreck until every vestige disappeared. He was not able to swim and death seemed imminent. As he sank in the sea, he promised the Blessed Virgin that if his life were spared he would devote every moment and every action of it to her.

At once he seemed lifted up, and as he rose to the surface he grasped a spar that floated near. Another survivor grasped the other end of it and began to curse most horribly. He was ordered to stop and to thank God for the chance to escape. Clinging to the plank, the two drifted for several hours. Then, when almost overcome with exhaustion, they were picked up. Young Price was believed to be dead, but restoratives brought him to, and he was able the next day to return to Wilmington and his family. The Star of the Sea, so fervently addressed in that hour of anguish, had come to the rescue of her loving son who, she knew, was to cultivate in his own soul and to propagate in the hearts of many others an especial devotion to her Immaculate Conception.

Owing to the consequences of a fever that followed upon the exposure and exhaustion, Frederick Price was unable to attend college at once. However, in February of the following year, he began his preparatory studies at St. Charles' College, Ellicott City, Maryland, where he continued as a student until his graduation in 1881. During those years financial hardships fell upon the family and they had to face many privations; but the brave and devoted mother made every sacrifice that her son might continue his preparation for the priesthood.

Shortly before receiving the subdiaconate, as a result of illness Frederick Price became deaf and he entertained great fears that this affliction would bar him from the priesthood. He immediately made a novena to the Blessed Virgin, and at its close his deafness left him, never again to return.

On September 12, 1881, he entered St. Mary's Seminary, Baltimore, for the study of philosophy, scripture, and theology. On May 30, 1885, he received subdeaconship from the Most Reverend James Gibbons, D.D., Archbishop of Baltimore, who, as a young priest, had labored among the people of the Carolinas and whose Mass Frederick Price had often served in his native town of Wilmington.

Meantime, however, his mother's health had been failing. Although it had been her dearest wish and her constant prayer that she should live to see her son ascend the altar, God ordained otherwise, for she died in August, 1885. There is good reason to believe that she quickly passed into the realm of the blessed, there to be nearer her priestly son, and more powerful in her prayers for

CLARISSA BOND PRICE, MOTHER OF
FATHER PRICE

him, than she could ever have been on earth. Theirs was the communion of the saints, intensified in a mutual and absolute devotion to the Immaculate Conception.

That her intercession availed much before the throne of God can be gathered from the following incidents. Father Moore, Mrs. Price's pastor and a very holy man, had become partially paralyzed and blind, so that he could no longer read Mass but had to content himself reciting the prayers he knew by heart. Shortly before her death, he said to her: " Mrs. Price, you will soon be with Almighty God, and when you see Him I want you to ask Him to give me my eyesight so that I may be able to read the Holy Masses." The morning after she died, he opened the Missal and read the Mass for the day. He then went to the family and told them not to grieve for Mrs. Price, as she was with God. Not long afterwards, Mrs. Price's little grandson, eight years old, was at Mass with his mother. Suddenly he screamed and fainted and had to be taken out of the church.

On becoming conscious he exclaimed, " O Mamma, I saw Grandma! She was sitting over the high altar, and a man sitting on one side and a beautiful lady on the other side, all dressed in spangles. And, O Mamma, Grandma was so pretty! " Pope Pius IX, through the venerable and learned Doctor Corcoran, pronounced the Price family, " the holy family."

On December 19, 1885, Frederick Price received deaconship from Archbishop Gibbons. The following summer he returned to his native city, Wilmington, and on June 30, 1886, was ordained by the Right Reverend H. P. Northrop, D.D., Vicar-Apostolic of North Carolina. Two other candidates were ordained at the same time. Father Price was the first North Carolinian to become a priest.

II

NORTH CAROLINA MISSION

II

NORTH CAROLINA MISSION

*T*HE new priest was not long blessed with the privileges of curacy. The pastor, Father Patrick Moore, having been given a vacation to visit his old home in Ireland that summer, Father Price was left in charge of the parish during his absence, and on his return was assigned to work in the rural districts. His early missionary days were spent over the whole eastern section of the state, east of Raleigh and north of Wilmington, a district of about three hundred square miles. He was once introduced in St. Mary's Seminary, Baltimore, by Abbé Magnien, in this way: "Gentlemen, behold the secular clergy of North Carolina!"

In 1888, Father Price was placed in charge of St. Paul's Church, New Bern, North Carolina, and its seventeen or more attached missions. Included in these towns was Golds-

boro, where there was no church but an
excellent and valuable lot purchased by his
predecessor, Reverend J. J. Reilly. Father
Price at once set about the difficult task of
building a church.

Those were days of intense prejudice
against everything Catholic, and he had only
a handful of Catholics to assist him, yet he
inaugurated a fair. His personality soon won
many friends for the cause so close to his
heart, especially among the Jewish citizens
of Goldsboro, who generously supported
him. In fact, the Jewish workers so out-
numbered the Catholics that a prominent
Hebrew gentleman advanced the question:
" Is this a Jew fair or a Catholic fair? " The
enterprise netted the truly phenomenal sum
of $1600. Friends in Philadelphia also
came to Father Price's assistance, so that he
was able to erect his church, — an attractive
building, for years one of the few Catholic
churches made of brick in North Carolina.
At the time, Father Price was offered a
marble altar for the Goldsboro church by a

Northern lady, on the condition that she be permitted to name the church. Father Price announced that he could not allow any one to name his first church. This was his opportunity to express his great devotion to the Mother of God, and he called it *St. Mary's*.

Some of the hardships endured on the pioneer missions of North Carolina are revealed by the following facts. For years Father Price was wont to go by rail from Goldsboro to Mount Olive, where he would be met by a zealous lay helper, Mordecai Jones, a convert to the Faith, who would drive Father Price twenty-one miles to Newton Grove, where the two would remain from Saturday until Wednesday. Then they would travel by buggy twenty-seven miles to the country church of The Good Shepherd, situated in the wilds of Duplin County. This church had been dedicated by Bishop Gibbons with Father Price acting as altar boy at the ceremony.

After a two days' stay, Mordecai Jones' buggy would carry Father Price forty miles' distance to Chinquapin, where there was the nucleus of a Catholic settlement. At that point Father Price placed a lay teacher and built a small school. He used to stay with a poor family who occupied a two-room house made of logs plastered together with mud. In this cabin Father Price slept on sheepskins in place of a mattress. He celebrated Mass in the school.

Mordecai Jones relates that those long trips were made in mud and ice, and that at times both Father Price and himself suffered intense pain from the cold and inclement weather. On one occasion Father Price suggested the recitation of the rosary for the intention that they might escape freezing. From Chinquapin, Mordecai would drive Father Price fifteen miles to a railroad station, from which he, Mordecai, would travel the long distance to his home near the Church of the Good Shepherd alone.

Later on Father Price purchased a horse, which he left at Goldsboro and which he used in traveling the twenty-seven miles to

Newton Grove. This horse bore the name of *Nancy Hanks*. It was a difficult matter to start *Nancy*, and at times equally difficult to stop her. Father Price was accustomed to make purchases in Goldsboro for his Newton Grove parishioners, who lived eighteen miles from the nearest town, — Newton Grove itself being not a town but a thickly settled country section. Once he left Goldsboro with a large cargo, — coffee, sugar, calico, and a supply of church vestments. Father Price mounted the buggy and resorted to his usual feat of starting *Nancy* by having a by-stander throw sand in her mouth. She started at a terrific pace, and continued the entire journey with ugly vengeance. Finally, Father Price, the buggy, and *Nancy Hanks* reached Newton Grove. All else had been lost along the road, — a dozen bottles of altar wine, a cope and other vestments, not to mention the merchandise he had essayed to deliver.

Father Price in those days was devoted, tireless, energetic, gay, mortified, and a deep lover of holy poverty. He cared nothing for his own comfort, and had the stomach of a goat and a constitution of iron. He loved the poor and lowly. He catechised everywhere, followed up his neophytes in corn and cotton fields, instructed under trees, at fence corners, and on tree stumps, ate the coarsest of food with laughing relish, took a deep interest in the negroes, and always had the most contagious gaiety.

He understood Southern religious prejudices and limitations better, perhaps, than any other priest in America, and was respected by the most crude backwoodsmen as well as by the better class, although they had otherwise no use for anything Catholic. He made allowance for their prejudices and never resented their convictions about the Faith. They thought him a good man, although a Catholic, and felt that there was nothing stilted about him. They observed his careless and poor dress, and saw that he was not particular as to the size and shape of the hat he wore or the quality of his shoes, or bothered whether his trousers were of the required length and the latest mode. They agreed with him that razorback bacon with plenty of juice, gritty cornbread made with water, and coffee, were fit for anyone on earth. He entered into the affairs of hogs, corn, and cotton, as one to the manner born, and they realized that " Mr. Priest " was a " tar heel " like themselves. He was criticised for one fault only, — " he drove his horse too fast," so they said, and tore down the roads like a wild man, oblivious of the wonder of the slow-going country folk. He was after souls and wanted to get there.

It was often asserted by the backwoods congregations that " Priest Price " verily believed what he preached. There was nothing of the fashionable preacher about him. He was not eloquent and never went outside the themes of the plain Gospel to try to captivate the fancy of his audience. His language was grave and not dramatic, but it touched the thought of others, and his simple and poor life flashed on his hearers. They reckoned him a " powerful preacher," and, when they were in the mood, he preached as long as they wished, which was much over an hour. " Christ and Him Crucified " were his frequent subjects of inspiration, and something generous, honest, and sincere seemed to radiate from him. The most illiterate white or black people understood him. He impressed them with the ringing truths of eternal life that came from his lips. He gave them plenty to think about, and they did not forget the divine message when he had finished.

Besides the church at Goldsboro, Father Price built also those at Halifax and Nazareth, and enlarged the church at Newton Grove. While exercising the nominal rectorship of the Sacred Heart Church, Raleigh, to which he was appointed in 1895, he spent his time in giving missions to non-Catholics throughout the state, and in working up plans for his projected missionary activity.*

* The first aid Father Price obtained *ab externo* in carrying on these missions to non-Catholics in the Caro-

Recognizing the value of the apostolate of the press, Father Price decided that the written should supplement the oral word, and that an apologetic magazine would be a most effective means of removing doubt, superstition, and ignorance; developing a healthy curiosity about the Faith; securing a proper respect for the Catholic Church and its adherents; and so paving the way for conversions. The magazine would prepare the field; then missioners should go about, teaching, preaching, doing good, meeting the people personally, defending the Faith, and explaining its doctrines to the individual. The two-fold combination of a magazine that would reach all, and missioners who would reach each one, seemed to Father Price not only a logical, but the only, solution of the peculiar problem offered by the South. Burning with zeal for souls, eager to be about his Father's business, his enthusiasm was infectious and he had no difficulty secur-

linas was from the Apostolic Mission House at the Catholic University, Washington.

ing permission to make the first steps in his apostolic program.

Accordingly, the magazine, *Truth*, was started. At first it was printed from a Raleigh printery, but later the editor got an old printing machine and did the work, with poor help, in the kitchen of the rectory. The congregation used to help by donations, folding the magazine, securing subscriptions, and so forth. Often, like Bishop England, he had to do most of the labor connected with the publication, save that he did not actually set the type, as the great John of Charleston had to do. As the time for publication approached, Father Price could always be seen with bundles of manuscripts bulging from his coat-pockets as he raced to catch a train. He was never a minute ahead for a train, but somehow he always used to make it. Many a time he told how he used to catch trains in the country, between stations. He would run to the top of a hill near the track, and whistle and yell to the engineer. The engineer would bring the

FATHER PRICE AS A SEMINARIAN

train to a halt and wait for Father Price to get aboard. Then " the bell would whistle and off she'd go again."

Father Price corrected his manuscript and jotted down his ideas on trains, in the dim waiting-rooms of country stations, or by the faint and flickering light of an ill-smelling lamp in some shack on the missions. He never made a cent on the paper, save by its indirect appeal, and he sent free copies broadcast to enlighten the ignorant and convert the prejudiced. Generous souls who knew his unselfish aims usually came to the rescue and helped to pay the printing bills. It is undisputed that this journal brought light and faith into many isolated non-Catholic homes in the South and West, and had Father Price restricted his apostolic zeal to *Truth* alone, he would have served his generation well.

The second step in the apostolic program was more difficult, namely, the supplying of missioners who would cultivate the ground prepared by the press. Because of constant and ever-increasing demands in other sections of the country, it was obvious that no sufficient supply of priests could be secured from without the state. In the state, vocations were pitifully insufficient. After much thought and prayer, Father Price conceived the plan of establishing a Catholic orphanage and boys' school, where some day vocations might be found and developed.

The required permission being secured, the next steps were to determine the location and to secure the funds for the apostolic nursery. In 1897, after considering many sites, Father Price bought a large tract of land at the place now called *Nazareth,* and on Rosary Sunday, October, 1899, he took possession. The Sisters of Mercy from Belmont were his coadjutors in this establishment of an orphan asylum, — the first missionary work undertaken at that point.

The beginnings at Nazareth were very humble. The buildings were plain wooden farm houses and the furnishings were extremely simple. The orphan boys were the most abject specimens imaginable, but they were better off under the care of Sister Catherine Price and her devoted helpers than they would have been in their own natural surroundings. Things were very poor at Nazareth in its beginning, but love reigned. Father Price looked seedy, and the poor sisters' black habits were tattered and torn and patched, and stained with spots which would not come out. Their hands were red, and their knuckles and fingers enlarged with labor, but joy and prayer were in the air and happiness reigned supreme.

From those early days — open, no doubt, to criticism — great and difficult good has come. A magnificent tract of land had been secured, a beginning was made. The housing was almost as poor as at Bethlehem; but the splendid orphan asylum for boys that the Vicariate now has at Nazareth, with its English Gothic brick buildings and its tenant village scattered about, is the natural fruition of that work which Father Price started there twenty-three years ago.

In June, 1900, Father Price received his first assistant, in the person of Reverend Michael A. Irwin, just ordained. Father Irwin (now Pastor of Newton Grove, North Carolina) relates that he found at Nazareth a marvelous collection of the most pitiful children he had ever seen: puny, malformed, wretched little children, the poorest of the poor. Father Price, he said, had a " nose for the poor, a talent for finding the most needy." If God exalts the humble, what is now the glory of him who " emptied himself " to become the spiritual father of that pitiful brood that he managed, with smiling gaiety, to gather to himself on the hills of Nazareth?

The boys at Nazareth, after school hours, folded and cut the leaves of the magazine, *Truth,* which was printed there for several years.

In 1901 Father Price acquired a fine property on the other side of the road, and at once set about gathering funds for the erection of a church and what he planned to be the home of his Apostolate. For two years he was absent a great part of the time, soliciting funds in the North, where he met with marked success because of the universal admiration that his character and his cause commanded. The priests' house, or *Regina Apostolorum*, as it was called, was built in the winter of 1901–1902, and the church about six months later. Both structures were of brick. The church, of a fine design in " country Gothic," still stands, but the *Regina Apostolorum*, not satisfactory in lay-out, was destroyed by fire in the spring of 1906. Father Price at once began to build the fine fire-proof edifice that housed the Apostolate until his departure from North Carolina, and that now serves as a convent and orphan asylum.

In February, 1901, Father Price received his second assistant, Reverend William F. O'Brien (later pastor of the Immaculate Conception Church at Durham, North Carolina). Father O'Brien found in the cornerstone of the priests' house, when it was burned in 1906, the following letter, which Father Price had thought would not be read for many years:

This stone has been blessed by the Reverend Thomas F. Price, on April 21, 1902. The Right Reverend Leo Haid, O.S.B., D.D., was to have blessed it yesterday when blessing the cornerstone of the church, but omitted it through fatigue. All the children of the orphanage, thirty-two in number, participated, singing hymns, etc., as well as Fathers O'Brien, Irwin, and Thomas Stapleton. This building begins the manifestation of a design for a religious order which has been held through many years of toil, sacrifice, and prayer. If God blesses it to succeed (and may it fail if the Divine Majesty so desires!), it will cover every diocese of the globe.

This building is consecrated to the Queen of the Apostles, in consequence of a vow made by the writer to our loved Blessed Mother, that if it come to success it would be hers — named after her. May Jesus, the sweetest love of our hearts, be praised, adored, and forever blessed! May our loved Mother be praised and blessed forever!

T. F. PRICE

Finally, with over two score of neophytes (the most promising of the orphans, and other students) and the two assistant priests, Fathers Irwin and O'Brien, community life of the Apostolate began. There was an immense deal of fervor about the place, and a strict monastic rule was observed for several years, everything being done on the stroke of the bell from five to nine, and no idle bread being eaten.

In those crowded years numbers of missions were given to the country people, frequently for two weeks at a time, and the chapels were well-crowded by the non-Catholics. No work was ever more apostolic! Of the twenty-five or thirty young disciples at Nazareth many have become holy and fervent priests in other parts of the United States. They were confirmed in their apostolic zeal at Nazareth.

Seminarians would come down in the summer from Baltimore and Dunwoodie and do valiant work around the country. The chapels would be veritable spiritual camps, with pots, pans and cooking paraphernalia, bread and raw food to be cooked, a priest and several seminarians in attendance, and wagon and mules, blankets and mattresses. The seminarians would spread their mattresses at night on the floor, and cover their tired bodies with the blankets. Rising at a fixed hour, after the direction of their minds to God, they would shake out of doors their blankets and bedding, fold them, sweep up every particle of dust, wash and attire themselves, have regular meditation and morning prayer, sing High Mass at 8 o'clock, hear a sermon, breakfast under the trees at 9:30, go out among the country people, and return at 3:00, when dinner would be served. Services and a sermon to the people at 3:45; recreation from 5 to 6; a little spiritual reading; supper about 6:30 under the trees; big service of prayer, hymns, and sermons at 8:15; after services, talks with the people; night prayers about 9:30; then silence and bed. All this for two weeks at a time, with coarse but abundant food. The seminarians from the regular seminaries, as a rule, highly edified the people by their devout catechetical instructions.

To the pen of Reverend William B. Hannon of Asheville, North Carolina, we are indebted for the following vivid impressions of a visit to Nazareth:

I always found a charm in visiting Father Price at Nazareth. The place, built on an eminence, gave one a sense of expanse on coming out of the fenland of most parts of eastern North Carolina. One could see quite a distance and behold the sky and clouds from horizon to horizon. There was something reposeful about the whole establishment.

It was a bright day in late spring when I accompanied Father Price and two of his students to open a week's mission to non-Catholics, at a little mission church in Wake County. Large fleecy clouds floated in a blue sky, but the sun was warm. I had been spending a few days at Nazareth, and gladly consented to join in the good work. Some beds and household effects were placed in a farm wagon, and the two priests and two students took their seats and set out for the place of rendezvous.

The road was full of ruts, and the passengers received many a jolt on the way. We passed colored settlements, then quite new and curious in my eyes. The large farm horse went by fits and starts, creeping along at times at a snail's pace, and then galloping as fast as his cumbersome load would allow. It was a fairly picturesque route, past pine woods, where doves cooed lazily among the trees, and many plantations of white folks, who placidly gazed at "Priest Price" and his luggage and companions, or looked with wonder and suspicion on the advent of the Catholic folk of Nazareth, invading the undisturbed territory of their Protestant creed, whose conflicting and unsightly churches were seen in all directions. I do not know where such ugly churches are to be found as in the solid Protestant South, except in Wales.

We saluted the people as we passed, and some jerked back a nod of recognition over their shoulders, as if making an effort to return the salutation. The people are well schooled against Catholicism by their spiritual teachers, who revel in all the old exploded scandals and lies concerning the Church. It is easy to see the glint of dislike on their faces when they know that one is a Catholic or a priest. The Southern States are still the happy hunting grounds of illiteracy and prejudice.

I was rather disappointed on seeing the mission chapel or shack, called very appropriately after St. Teresa, who had to put up with such crude structures in her new reform establishments. It presented an interior of confusion, not having been used for months, but it soon changed its appearance. The mattresses were duly laid on the sacristy floor, where we were to sleep, and the novelty was pleasing to us. As for Father Price, he was unconscious of any difference, and was quite as at home in the poorest hut in the backwoods as in the most agreeable city home. One of the students, now a Superior in a religious order, went out to the natives, who were viewing from afar the invasion, and bargained with them for milk and other sundries, and so broke the ice.

Father Price, with his truly devotional spirit, was full of the fire of prayer and zeal, but it was a barren soil for converts. However, its spiritual distress was an appealing plea to his apostolic heart. I noticed during my sermon that men and women were continually spitting, and felt hurt at the profanity in a Catholic church, even in this poor shack.

My memories of that mission are half pleasant, half pathetic. That the large attendance was untouched, like many millions in the Sunny South, was the sad feature of Catholic failure to reach these people. They go through life in the old circumscribed familiar ways, knowing little of the Church of God, and, in fact, ignorant of the fundamental truths of Christianity; passing from youth to old age, and from the death-bed to the graveyard, missing so much certain hope that the Church gives the peasantry elsewhere. Such has been Catholic endeavor for generations. Even the great heart of Bishop England had to feel the same trial after all the torrents of his fervid eloquence, his poverty, his self-sacrifice, and the clouds of suspicion in which his open, generous nature had to be enveloped. It is recorded that this holy and gifted man made few converts in his day.

The following incident shows another phase of Father Price's work.

A negro, Henry Spivy, was tried and convicted at Elizabethtown, Bladen County, on the charge of arson and murder. He was carried to the State prison of Raleigh for safe keeping pending his appeal to the Supreme Court. Visiting the prison, as was Father Price's custom, he met the condemned man. The higher court refused a new trial, and Spivy was carried back to his home county, accompanied by Father Price, who stopped at Lumberton to interview the condemned man's lawyers in the hope of securing a short postponement of the hanging in order that he might give further religious instructions to the negro.

Father Price hired a horse and buggy and drove thirty miles to Elizabethtown in order to be with Spivy on the day appointed for the hanging. On the day originally appointed for the execution, thousands of people had assembled to witness this, the last public hanging in North Carolina. When the announcement was made of the postponement the people were in an ugly mood. Blame was charged to the Catholic priest present. Father Price appeared in the midst of the disappointed assemblage, confirmed the rumor that the hanging had been put off, and invited all to go with him to the Court House to hear a talk given by a Catholic priest. People packed the court-room, and his hearers expressed their admiration for the missioner and the impression made on them by his talk. After the labors of the day Father Price drove back the thirty miles to Lumberton.

A week later Father Price again made the difficult trip. On the night before the execution he requested that he be locked in the cell with the prisoner. This was done. It was noted by the jailers that while the negro spent his last night on earth in sound sleep, the other occupant of the cell passed the long hours in prayer. The next morning Father Price used a box as an altar, celebrated Mass, and gave Spivy Holy Communion. Spivy's was the last public legal hanging in North Carolina.

*FATHER PRICE IN HIS NORTH
CAROLINA DAYS*

It is no matter for wonder that all who were associated with Father Price, this truly apostolic and saintly man, loved him, and with his ardent zeal stirring their hearts strove hard for their own spiritual development and the glory of God.

As time went on, however, it became gradually evident that, despite all the means, natural and supernatural, taken to assure its success, the Apostolate was not destined to be permanent. Bitter as this realization must have been to the zealous apostle, meaning, as it then seemed, the ruin of his projected life-work, the blow was nevertheless accepted with the most perfect resignation, and Father Price's natural sweetness of temper and his infectious cheerfulness seemed in no degree affected. He had begun the work thinking it to be God's will. He regarded its apparent failure, despite his best efforts and prayers, as a manifestation of God's will; and, while his apostolic heart bled for the countless souls that he had hoped to reach through the Apostolate, he was wholly resigned to the inscrutable designs of Providence.

Several reasons conspired to defeat Father Price's plan of a religious order for the South, but we may say, in a word, that he was so overwhelmed with the labor of building and money-getting that he could not give to the rising Society the minute attention it demanded. His labors were gigantic, since he had to be superior, builder, money-getter, editor, and missioner, all in one. Then, too, in his ardent zeal he wanted big results quickly. Had he gone more slowly and deliberately, and been satisfied with less progress at first, his success might have been greater. These, however, are merely natural reasons for what then appeared the failure of one of Father Price's projects. None of his works should be judged according to human standards, but by divine. Regarded thus, they were not failures, but only the means whereby the soul of our apostle was being prepared and strengthened, by experience and grace, for still greater things.

III
MARYKNOLL APOSTOLATE

III

MARYKNOLL APOSTOLATE

WHILE at the Eucharistic Congress in Montreal, in September, 1910, Father Price met his future associate, Father Walsh, then Archdiocesan Director, in Boston, of the Society for the Propagation of the Faith. Each was deeply interested in apostolic work, each had heard of and was eager to meet the other. It was the special grace of God that brought both together at the Eucharistic Congress.

When two souls animated by the same spirit and purpose come together, it is to be expected that they should desire and plan to join forces. Such was the decision of these two apostolic workers, and then and there was conceived the idea of supplying what they considered America's greatest spiritual need, a national foreign mission seminary, which would not only take away our reproach among the nations — that we were a people ignoring apostolic obligation — but would also, as in the case of Holland, react spiritually in stimulating needed vocations for religious work at home.

The following May, encouraged and authorized by the unanimous approbation of the American hierarchy in response to a letter sent out by Cardinal Gibbons, of Baltimore, Father Price went with Father Walsh to Rome, to secure approval for the new work.

This approval was granted on June 29, the Feast of Saints Peter and Paul; and the following day the Holy Father, Pius X, received Father Price and Father Walsh in private audience, at the close of which His Holiness blessed the work and its organizers.

A few days later Father Price left Rome for Lourdes, the spot on earth that he desired most to visit, because of his intense love for the Immaculate Conception and for her little protegée, Bernadette Soubirous. He stayed with the brother of Bernadette, visited the convent where she had lived and died, was favored with the gift of some treasured souvenirs, and established a warm friendship with her relatives that endured until death.

Up to this time Father Price had continued as owner and editor of *Truth*. Father Walsh had also been publishing *The Field Afar*, a bi-monthly magazine devoted to apostolic work in pagan lands. As the purpose of the new national Seminary was exclusively foreign mission, it was now considered unfeasible either to continue each separately, or to merge the two magazines, and Father Price accordingly severed his connection with *Truth*, putting it into the hands of persons who, he judged, would carry it on in accord with his ideals.

In December, 1911, Father Price went with Father Walsh to the home of the Dominican Fathers at Hawthorne, New York, and, making this his headquarters, entered energetically upon the second and more immediate step in founding the foreign mission seminary — the launching of a campaign of propaganda to arouse vocations and to secure financial support for the training and maintenance of missioners. While Father Walsh, chosen Superior of the Seminary, remained in Hawthorne, and later in Ossining, New York, to direct the correspondence and to supervise the rapidly growing institution, Father Price covered practically every diocese in the East, speaking in churches, convents, seminaries, colleges, schools, hospitals, wherever he could find the opportunity, to picture the appalling conditions in pagan lands, to request prayers, to encourage vocations, to find friends for the new work.

His wide acquaintance, developed on propaganda for the North Carolina mission, and the high regard in which he was held by his many friends among the clergy and laity of the country, were invaluable to the new work in winning friends and help in its early and critical stage. May we not ascribe to the labors and zeal of Father Price no inconsiderable share in the rapid growth of Maryknoll — a development all the more remarkable by reason of its occurring at a time when the

Great War dealt severely with unrelated projects?*

As the intervals between propaganda trips became longer, Father Price was more constantly associated with the Seminary work as Spiritual Director of the students. Here his influence was particularly happy. The students, realizing his ardent though unpretentious sanctity, could not but admire and aspire to such zeal as had kept aflame his mission enthusiasm during his long and trying career in the South and that now prompted him to go to pagan lands to spend and be spent for Christ. His unfailing good humor communicated itself to all hearts, making light the unmistakable hardships of Maryknoll's early days. His influence helped to crystallize one of the most impressive and

* When Father Price left for China, in September, 1918, the Maryknoll institution counted seventeen ordained priests, seventy-five students for the priesthood, ten auxiliary brothers and thirty sisters, while substantial accommodation for all had been provided at the Maryknoll center in Ossining, New York, and at the Preparatory College in Clarks Summit, a suburb of Scranton, Pennsylvania.

precious traits of the " Maryknoll spirit," a heaven-sent cheerfulness that makes every yoke sweet and every burden light when borne for the love of God and man.

Being thus an edification to all, particularly to his penitents, whom he directed with an eye ever keen to perceive and follow God's designs — as they now so gratefully testify — Father Price might have been considered settled in the final work of a busy life. But God seemed to have further plans for an instrument so useful, for he was destined to become a vital factor in giving to the actual workers in the mission field the direction, the spirit, and the tradition that have already reaped a glorious spiritual harvest and won encomiums of praise from other and more seasoned missioners.

In 1918 when the Maryknoll Seminary Council decided to send four priests to the mission, Father Price manifested his desire to go, in spite of the anticipated difficulties of climate and language, difficulties that were serious for one of his age.

The desire and the zeal to do missionary work in the field afar, to suffer its privations and to bear in patience the rigors and hardships that fall to the lot of every missionary priest and nun, is a thing to be admired in young men and women; but when a man who is fast approaching three-score starts on a missionary career to a distant country to labor for the salvation of souls and the alleviation of the sufferings of a people whose customs, manners, and habits are strange to him, and whose climate promises keenest physical suffering, then we can truly say that such a man is filled with an apostolic zeal that is almost divine.

On the eighth of September, 1918, Feast of the Nativity of the Blessed Virgin Mary, Father Price, in company with three Maryknoll priests, Fathers James E. Walsh, Francis X. Ford, and Bernard F. Meyer, left Maryknoll for China. Then began the third period of Father Price's missionary activity. He was spared to the missioners, his companions, but a little over a year, yet even in that short time his presence proved an invaluable aid to those pioneers. The Bishop of Canton and his priests at first felt that a mistake had been been made in sending a priest of Father Price's age, but when they knew him better they wrote: " His coming was an inspiration."

For the last chapter in the life of this saintly and heroic priest, we have the official report made after his death by Father James E. Walsh, his successor as Superior of the Maryknoll Mission in China. Father Walsh's statement runs as follows:

Having decided to throw himself personally into actual missionary work, Father Price determined to leave no stone unturned that could aid him in becoming a successful missioner and above all in guiding the destinies of the newly launched mission. It was with this motive that he included in his itinerary a trip through some of the missions of Japan, Korea and Northern China, where he talked with the bishops and missioners, noted methods, and picked up ideas in regard to the work.

Arriving at Canton in November, after a short stay at the Cathedral to get the instructions of Bishop de Guébriant, under whom we were to work, Father Price with Father Gauthier and his three confrères went directly to Yeungkong, the tentative center of the new American Mission, where all settled down to the humdrum of learning the Chinese language and picking up notions about the practical prosecution of mission work.

Yeungkong was Father Price's first and only mission in China. During the year that God gave him to spend here, he made several trips to Canton and Hongkong on business connected with the mission, but those trips were only a matter of a few weeks, and all the rest of his time was passed at Yeungkong.

Father Price was fifty-eight years old when he came to China. He was evidently beyond the age when a man can accustom himself to a new and deleterious climate, and the change was for him particularly severe for, being a sufferer from rheumatism, he found that ailment acutely intensified by the extreme humidity of Southern China. In addition, there is something about the life and climate of this country that is very wearing on the nerves, and Father Price's nervous

condition during this time was a matter of alarm
to both himself and his confrères. Perhaps it
was accentuated by his dogged perseverance
in studying the Chinese language, a nerve-racking
performance at best, and a task that becomes
almost superhuman for a man of his age. Nothing could prevail upon him to give it up, nor even
to let up on the severe course he had mapped out
for himself.

During his short career he had little chance to
do any actual mission work, as he was never able
to make himself understood in Chinese, that being impossible for any one in so short a time.
Yet he went through the regular initiation of the
young novice, going out on the mission trips to
points around Yeungkong, often traveling in the
most primitive conditions, and putting up with
all sorts of hardships with as little concern as the
youngest and strongest of us. Added to that,
even the daily life at Yeungkong was not so pleasant, for everything was rough and cave-man
fashion, and many things that Americans learn to
look upon as necessaries of life were simply not
to be had. *Through it all Father Price was his
serene, gentle self, never complaining, never out
of patience, even at times when the others were*

ST. THOMAS' CHURCH, WILMINGTON, NORTH CAROLINA

Here Father Price was baptized, served as an altar-boy, and was ordained.

frankly dissatisfied. He gave an example that will long be remembered by those who had the good fortune to be associated with him at this time.

As to Father Price's private spiritual life, it was what everyone who ever knew him anywhere has had the privilege of seeing — one of great recollection and union with God in prayer, and it was perhaps intensified by his stay in China. He saw *many things that cried out to his zeal, and being without the means of doing any personal work, or even, in so short a time, of making any plans for the extension of the mission's activity, he always turned to his rosary, where he would ask God for the results he so ardently desired.* To the young priests who were with him, his spirit of prayer, his gentleness, and his zeal were a constant revelation. They seemed to see some new evidence of these qualities every day, so as to make them feel that they had not rightly known the man before.

It was a curious thing that Father Price was able to make the impression that he did on the Chinese. Certainly he was never able to manage the simplest conversation in Chinese; the most we ever heard him say were the two sentences, "How are you?" and "God bless you!" But the Chinese with whom he came in contact were attracted to Father Price. They liked him, and they said so; it was a known fact at the mission that Father Price was extremely popular with them. It is worth mentioning, also, that *the Chinese commonly referred to him as " the holy priest."* There was a something about him that it did not need language to convey, and these simple people felt it.

Father Price had little time or opportunity to become well acquainted with our French confrères, but the impression he made upon them was always good. He did not have sufficient command of French to permit a real exchange of ideas, but they got enough from him to realize the character of the man, and all of them who met him expressed their conviction that Father Price was a beautiful character and a man of sanctity far out of the ordinary. Even the lay people he met here appreciated him. One Protestant doctor, on being asked to remember Father Price in his prayers, said, " No use — he was a saint."

Father Price died at St. Paul's Hospital, Hongkong, where he had gone from Yeungkong to be operated on for appendicitis. The operation was a clean-cut one, but he did not have sufficient vitality to react. He died September 12, 1919, on the Feast of the Holy Name of Mary. He was buried on the following morning at Happy Valley Cemetery in Hongkong. The grave was blessed by Bishop Pozzoni, and many priests and religious were in attendance, among them Fathers Gauthier and Deswazières, who represented the mission of Canton.

No Maryknoller was at the bedside of Father Price when he died, and none was present at the obsequies. It could not be; yet God provided a substitute in the person of a devoted friend of Maryknoll, Father Jean Tour of the Paris Seminary, who wrote these details of the last hours:

Maryknoll-in-China was already founded on the virtues, the apostolic zeal, and the strenuous labors of the first missioners you sent out here one year ago. This is, I think, your anniversary day, a good and very good day, indeed, the Feast of the Most Holy Name of Mary. To-day, at precisely 10:10 A.M., your young Mission has received its second consecration and a lasting blessing, by the happy and holy death of the venerable

57

and saintly Father Price. What we feared yesterday is now a sad reality.

The good Father did not feel well yesterday. He passed a good night, but at three this morning awoke feeling unwell again. At seven he asked for the Last Rites. He told me there was no hurry, that he could wait for me, but he insisted upon receiving Holy Viaticum, Extreme Unction, and the Plenary Indulgence.

Father Lemaire, a missioner of Canton, who is a convalescent there, yielded to his wish, and all the Rites were received in the most edifying manner.

When I arrived at nine, good Father Price gave me a sweet smile and a hearty handshake. He spoke very low, but quite intelligibly. I helped him the best way I could during the hour. His hands and forehead were cold. Had it not been for that, we should have felt no anxiety for the day. He was very quiet and even somewhat hopeful. Still, there was no doubt but that he was sinking. I spoke to him of all things dear to him: of Jesus, Mary, Joseph, of Our Lady of Lourdes, of Bernadette, and he was smiling and giving assent all the while. Then, of Father Walsh, and of all the beloved Maryknollers,

Maryknoll proper, Scranton, San Francisco, Yeungkong. At each name he lifted his head heavenward and prayed according to the thoughts and intentions I suggested.

At about nine-thirty, I understood that he was sinking more speedily. " Dear Father Price, you will kindly bless your friend, Father Tour, and, in his person, dear Father Walsh and all beloved Maryknollers of Maryknoll, Scranton, San Francisco, and Yeungkong, won't you? "

" Most willingly and from the depth of my heart," he replied.

" You offer now your sufferings, and even your life, for the prosperity of your beloved Society, and you pray and will ever pray that they all may do the work of God in a truly apostolic spirit, don't you? "

" Most certainly."

And as I bowed before him by the side of his bed, he placed his weak hand on my head and blessed me, making the Sign of the Cross on me and praying at the same time, as I guessed, the blessing formula.

Up to nine-forty-five he repeated all the ejaculations after me, but his tongue was no more free. Until then he always gently smiled at the Holy

59

Names and the names of Maryknoll. I started the prayers for the Commendation of the Soul, in English, which he seemed to follow throughout. When these prayers were over, he could see no more. Then he felt very distressing pain in his wound and moved pitifully to the right and to the left a dozen times, while his breath was more and more hard and scarce. At ten, he opened wide and wild eyes and was shaken most painfully. The good Sister on one side and I on the other helped him the best we could, holding his hand until he breathed his last quite peacefully, after some five minutes' rest.

I had the sad privilege of closing the eyes of your venerable friend and devoted co-operator in the great work of Maryknoll. I felt that I was representing you all, and I could not stop my tears. I can assure you that his death was in the very truth the death of a just man, and even of a saint. His last words were: "Tell Father Walsh my last thoughts were for them all, and that I died in the love of Jesus, Mary, Joseph, and of Maryknoll."

More than one has seen in his death a re-semblance to that of St. Francis Xavier. In some ways it was very dissimilar. The Saint died on the opposite shores of Sancian Island, amid the most primitive surroundings, while Father Price died in a modern hospital, surrounded by several priests and religious. But primitive or modern surroundings do not make much difference when it is a question of dying, and Father Price, like Saint Francis, died far from his homeland, his kith and kin, his friends, laying down his life in the strange country that he had come to evangelize. His memory will be held in benediction, and his prayers from Heaven will help to sustain the work that he inaugurated among his brethren who sit in darkness and the shadow of death.

What an appropriate and long novitiate Father Price had in his own homeland for the Chinese mission of his last year on earth! He accepted whatever God sent, and recognized that he had to plough the furrows and wait for God to give success or failure. He never repined, but did his utmost and was cheerful at small results or none at all.

61

His life was unpretentious and far from the beaten path, unheralded and unrewarded as far as the world goes. He could not have begun work in a more disappointing field of the Church than in North Carolina; he could hardly have faced heavier trials than those that awaited him in China; but that did not cause him to float feebly upon the Will of God like a branch that spins around in a whirlpool. Oftentimes he had abundant cause to be weary and sad, but he shared those trying experiences as well as his joys with God.

His life as a missioner in one of the most Protestant states in the Union had been one of innumerable deeds of suffering, resignation, love, and humility. These grew in number and sublimity, and the end of his life in heathen China, as old age came upon him, is the striking evidence of how beloved he was in Heaven. He could say in China, as in North Carolina if the ghostly visitant had reached him there: " Bonum certamen certavi, cursum consummavi, fidem servavi."

When news of Father Price's death reached America, *Truth* (the magazine which he had founded as the organ of his work in the South), wrote of him:

A good man and a brave man and a rare man left this poor world when Father Price breathed his last, like Francis Xavier, in far-off China. Though not possessed of great mental gifts, he nevertheless accomplished a great work through sheer zeal and pluck and prayer. His life was divided into two periods, spent at opposite sides of the earth.

The first period was taken up with his priestly labors in North Carolina, and truly they were the labors of an apostle burning with zeal for the salvation of souls. When he began them, some forty years ago, the conditions were enough to discourage a veritable Paul. Those conditions consisted of the abysmal ignorance of, and colossal antipathy towards, Catholicity on the part of North Carolinians. The life of a priest was then and there one that called for unusual courage and strength of character. Laborers in more fruitful portions of the Lord's Vineyard can hardly realize the difficulties of priests placed as Father Price was. He had, it is true, a little parish, — little in numbers, but vast in extent, and it was often his lot to get from town to town or up among the mountains and into the woods with a pack on his back, sleeping sometimes by the wayside or in hayricks, begging a meal here and there — sometimes the meal being refused. Yet the young apostle stuck to his work, not only manfully, but always with even cheerfulness. Food, clothing and all such bodily comforts simply meant nothing to him.

We owe to his foresight the creation of *Truth*, which now numbers among its subscribers over 120,000, dwelling in every State in the Union. In a way it did take a sort of genius to create all this. Certainly, it took a rare man to conceive and carry it through to success. How he did succeed is a marvel, because he succeeded with nothing. Disaster in the form of fire that destroyed the plant erected by long and arduous toil, lack of funds, criticism — nothing daunted him. Under his guidance the little magazine leaped into a characteristic place in religious journalism and has ever been a source of enlightenment to non-Catholics and of assistance to Catholics. It was rare instinct that made of him a veritable pioneer in sensing the power of the press for defending the Church; all the more remarkable when we reflect that he had no traditions in such matters to guide him.

Father Price's yearning for the foreign missions was born chiefly from a genuine desire to " go the limit " of apostolic self-sacrifice. Unknown but to a few special friends, his desire was to actually lay down his life for the Faith, so that he prayed for martyrdom. Had he lived in the early youth of Christianity he would have become a Sebastian or a Pancratius. Later on he would have joined a Patrick or a Boniface. As it was, he imitated a Francis Xavier. His death over there by the rising sun is a significant event, for it is the first of any missioner sent there by a distinctly American foreign missionary society. Perhaps it marks, in its humble way, the turn of the world on its spiritual axis — the turn from West to East. The history of Christianity — in fact, of civilization — has been these three or four thousand years a steady turning of East to West, from the Euphrates through Athens to Rome, to Paris, to London, to New York, to San Francisco. And now, it perhaps is beginning to retrace its progress, by crossing the Pacific and touching to life the dormant millions of China.

It is not a peevish pessimism of limited view, but rather the big optimism of a world-wide vision, that looks with hope to the East as it now contemplates the spiritual ruins of civilization in the West. Our own civilization is tottering under its burden of materialism. It cannot endure as it is at present. It has the symptoms of the decay that overcame Rome in the days of Pompey and the early Caesars. Then the new life blossomed out again amidst the virgin soil by the Rhine and the Seine and the Thames. Centuries later, old Europe received a new stimulant after Columbus found a yet fresher soil across the Atlantic. But, now, there is no more a new soil. Civilization — that is, spiritual civilization — must return to the old neglected fields that perhaps lie on the slopes of the Himalayas or on the banks of the Yangtse, where the brutality of modern machinery has not yet clubbed the spirit of man into servitude. The East calls the missioner now, as the West called him long ago. But it is ever the same call. . . . And so, perhaps, Father Price's going into the dawn, and his death at the shining portals of the East, may after all mark in a humble way the beginning of something new and fresh in the world's history. It may be as the gentle moving of the early dawn's air, ere

THE MARYKNOLL MISSION COMPOUND, YEUNGKONG, 1919

The chapel is marked by a cross at left. It is under the patronage of Our Lady of Lourdes.

the fresher morning wind sings its matins to the rising sun. He is not to be mourned. We can well say of him, as we say of the saints, that his feast-day is the day of his death. That day of his has about it all the glory of the morning, and the promise of new life. — *Truth.*

IV

THE MAN OF GOD

IV

THE MAN OF GOD

IN thinking of Father Price, one always
pictures him far removed from the
noise and strife of the crowd. His struggles
were set in quiet places: he sought his own
soul's sanctification in the prayer and dis-
cipline of solitude, and the salvation of
others in the hills and dales of his North
Carolina mission and later in the remote
mission-fields of China. Maryknoll, situated as it is on a fine eminence, looking
out upon the stately Hudson, and still
clothed in much of its primeval beauty,
afforded him every opportunity for seclu-
sion, and his was a familiar figure, clothed in
an ancient well-patched cassock, long black
cloak that he had received from the brother
of his beloved Bernadette of Lourdes, and
old soft hat, as, with head and shoulders
bowed and rosary in hand, he strode through

71

the compound, clambering over stone walls until he was finally lost in the wooded groves. Thence he emerged hours later: and the supreme joy on his countenance, and the tell-tale stains on his cassock, of which he was unconscious, revealed the secret of the precious time spent on his knees in heavenly communion with Jesus and Mary, whose knight he was.

Father Price was strongly, almost ruggedly, built and of robust health, except for severe attacks of rheumatism, contracted, doubtless, from exposure to all kinds of weather and lack of proper food while in the Carolina mission. He was heard to say that he had more than once slept in open fields or in barns, when other shelter had been refused him by the natives. In the *Life of Madame Rose Lummis*, herself an apostle of the South, we read:

He went from town to town, preaching in the market-place and being plied with questions, which he desired, but often with cabbages and worse, which he did not desire, before he won a hearing on the claims of the Catholic Church. Undaunted, he continued his way. He slept anywhere and everywhere, ate what he got, and went about distributing literature broadcast. The seed fell here and there; his ambition for souls was boundless.

Ordinarily quick and somewhat nervous in action, he was slow and deliberate in everything pertaining to serious problems and religious matters. His kind blue eyes — often lighted with a merry twinkle, for he had a keen, delightful sense of humor — his genial winning smile, and his evident gentleness, made him so approachable that even strangers speedily felt at ease with him. This accessibility was strengthened by his manner. No matter how preoccupied he was, he would drop everything, with no appearance of reluctance, to hear whatever one had to say, giving his attention with such sympathy and understanding that very often the mere recital of a difficulty would seem to solve it.

Wide experience, rare discernment, and excellent judgment, combined with natural charm, made Father Price a welcome addition to any circle. His fund of anecdotes, both serious and amusing, seemed inexhaustible, and there was hardly a topic that he could not illustrate most entertainingly from his own experience. Father Tabb, the blind poet-priest of St. Charles' College, and Abbé Magnien of St. Mary's Seminary, were frequently the subjects of such stories; but no tales were more delightful than those, related in his rich Southern drawl, of the " po' whites " and the negroes among whom he had labored.

Father Price was universally beloved. He was full of tenderness and loving kindness for all the frail beings of the world, and even some most rigorous Protestants admired his truly Catholic charity and became his sincere friends. He had sufficient breadth of mind to empty himself and become all in all to the poor backward Southern white man, and at the same time learning and manners enough not to be despised by the polished Southern gentlemen. A priest who worked with him in the South declares that " the two

classes are poles apart, and Father Price
could face either pole perfectly. He was
always *persona grata* to the Southern gentry.
There was nothing crude about him, although
he was perfectly unconscious of the quality
of his food and clothing and quite at home
in the poorest and roughest surroundings."

He was not long engaged in the ministry
when his ability as a missioner was recognized, and he was called upon for difficult
missions, until finally he was allowed by the
bishop to devote himself to the conversion
of his Southern non-Catholic countrymen.
He quietly exerted an influence upon the
most illiterate and prejudiced: he was verily
a good shepherd to the lost and sinful ones:
and he thought no soul for whom Christ
died outside the range of his pastoral care.
He was never so cramped and selfish as to
think that his work was within the confines
of a particular territory, and that souls elsewhere had no claim on him: his zeal was
truly Catholic, not parochial. He looked to
souls, and, like the celebrated Father of the

Church, reckoned one soul worthy the ministry of a bishop. He would preach to two colored children as earnestly as if they were a whole congregation: and he counted it nothing to go twenty miles across the mountains to receive into the Church a single convert.

Humility, practiced in an heroic degree, was an outstanding trait of Father Price's character. He was forever preaching it, and he lived according to his precepts. Convinced that it is the very foundation of the spiritual life, Father Price tried to impress upon the students the great principle that without humility everything is founded on quicksand. At every spiritual reading which he conducted when at Maryknoll he endeavored to inculcate in the students some of his own regard for this virtue.* He seldom spoke of himself, or of his work in North Carolina, beyond narrating some humorous incident, and he disliked very much having

* In doing this, he made constant use of the Exercises of St. Ignatius, and in particular of the teachings

anyone else mention it. He absolutely forbade Father Walsh to put his name in *The Field Afar*, or to make any reference to him — much to the bewilderment of his many friends, who would occasionally inquire about his " disappearance." He would never consent to having his picture taken, even in a group, but in spite of this an occasional " snap " was secured by cleverly aimed cameras. (Fortunately, he waived this ironclad rule before leaving for China, and some pictures taken at that time show him in a characteristic mood.) He always tried to take the last place at table and to be the last in leaving a room. He took care of his own room, making the bed and sweeping and dusting. He was indifferent to his clothing, which was frequently " hand-me-downs " from some

on humility of the great Jesuit. In his younger days, Father Price had desired to be a Jesuit, and for some time was faced with the choice of missionary work among the non-Catholics of North Carolina, or of becoming a Jesuit religious. On the advice of his confessor he had definitely given up the latter idea, but he always had a strong admiration for the famous Order and the spiritual advice of its saintly founder.

of his former classmates, and to his food with one exception: he refused to eat apples in any form. Why? Because they were the forbidden fruit of Paradise, and the medium by which sin was brought into the world.

If Father Price's dress and oddities were sometimes amusing, if his constant preaching of humility ever seemed overdrawn, we must look upon them as foils which show in greater luster the sterling spirituality of the man. Whether one takes sanctity as " regularity, punctuality, and exactness," or whether it is considered as " being one with God in thought, in love, and in action," Father Price was a man of evident and pre-eminent holiness, a holiness attained by the yielding of his body to mortifications and his soul to the inspirations of the Holy Ghost. The following incident — and we could give many others — is related by a priest for some time associated with Father Price in his North Carolina mission work:

He called me once in a hurry to hear his edifying confession, and just as I had given him absolution

ST. MARY'S CHURCH, GOLDSBORO,
NORTH CAROLINA

The first church built by Father Price.

he was about to put me playfully out of the room when a sudden call came by telephone, and he had to rush to answer it. I hurriedly took in the surroundings of the cell-like room, and pulled the blanket from the bed where he slept, as it looked devoid of a mattress. I then saw that he slept on the bars, which must have pained his side and ribs. He evidently recollected that he had left me behind in the room and rushed impetuously back. I banteringly told him that he should be ashamed to do such violence to his flesh, and he replied that I should not have satisfied my curiosity by uncovering the bed. He demanded silence on the subject, which I now break. I realized that we have not passed the days of the great saints even in this worldly age, and felt a hope for the conversion of pitiful men when choice souls like the poor missioner of North Carolina prayed and suffered for them.

At first Father Price was too enthusiastic in his corporal penances and his health and strength suffered. On the advice of his director he later modified these austerities and sought sanctity in unswerving fidelity to a rule of life. Whether at work or prayer,

79

Father Price showed the same untiring zeal. On his propaganda tours he worked at top speed, and in the home nest at Maryknoll, where he devoted himself chiefly to writing, his concentration was admirable.

From his rising in the morning until his retiring at night, Father Price's life seemed to be one of uninterrupted union with God. Even in his busiest hours he lived in an " atmosphere " of heaven, and whenever the opportunity offered he would be on his knees before the little shrine of Our Lady in his room, or in the chapel before the Blessed Sacrament. In his absent-mindedness he forgot *things,* but never the presence of God. He always found time for spiritual reading and recollection, and this without neglecting the demands of an intensely active apostolate. In all seasons, the late hours of the night and the early dawn found him wrapped in prayer. At Maryknoll the sacristan often found in the chapel the stump of a candle that had been burned during the night; yet at the first sound of the bell

Father Price would rise again for morning prayer and meditation. Mass he said very devoutly, in about thirty-five minutes. It was his custom to spend considerable time in making the Mementos. After Mass, usually said at the Blessed Virgin's altar, he would make his thanksgiving at the altar and then follow it with the Stations of the Cross. During the day he said the Little Office of the Blessed Virgin, and he strongly urged his penitents to cultivate the same devotion. While he talked, or listened, or walked, or rode, his rosary was present, twined about his fingers during conversation, or slipping between them as he told the decades. A man of prayer, he found real companionship and genuine spiritual pleasure in the mere "feel" of his rosary. He must have said it a dozen times a day. If a visitor opened the door of his room too quickly after the cheery, "Come in!" he was likely to surprise Father Price scrambling from his knees before the little shrine, rosary in hand, and looking embarrassed at being "caught".

A priest in Jersey City recalls Father Price's visit to his church one Sunday some years ago. On that occasion, after hearing Father Price's mild appeal for *Field Afar* subscriptions at the first Mass, this priest became anxious and said to him in the sacristy, "Father Price, do you depend on your sermon for your propaganda results?"

Father Price smiled and replied, "Why do you ask?"

And his friend answered: "I want to see you make good. But if you don't put more strength into your appeal your visit here will be fruitless."

Father Price thanked his host, and told him that in reality he depended especially on prayer. And the priest, in telling of the incident, added, "He took away the largest sum of money ever gathered by any missioner visiting our church."

Father Price's greatest spiritual joy was to honor Our Immaculate Mother, to whom he rendered a devotion that for its depth and constancy was remarkable; and inseparable

from this love, and born of it, was his great
devotion to Bernadette Soubirous, his " little
saint ", the " Lily of Mary ".   On the feast
days of either Our Blessed Mother or Bernadette, Father Price (who was especially
pleased to be called " Father Bernadette ")
would go off for the day, making a retreat
to some shrine of Mary Immaculate, where
he would spend hours in uninterrupted
prayer.   The first seeds of this devotion had
doubtless been planted by his mother, who
had a great love for The Immaculate Conception; and his escape from drowning, through
her intercession as he believed, as well as his
relief from deafness after a novena in her
honor, surely strengthened it.   Gratitude
and love prompted him to do all in his power
to honor Our Blesed Lady and to secure for
her greater reverence and affection in the
hearts of others.   The churches that he
erected in North Carolina were named for
her, — the *Church of The Immaculate Conception* at Halifax and *St. Mary's* at Goldsboro.   His priests' house was called *Regina*

Apostolorum: and had his religous order for
the South been successful it would have been
dedicated to her, also. Whenever the Ordo
allowed a votive Mass, Father Price would
invariably read the Mass of The Immaculate
Conception of December 8; and on those
occasions this man, who never wore anything
but the poorest personal clothing, would in-
sist on having the very best vestments in the
Seminary.

We are reminded here of an incident that
occurred on the day of Father Price's departure for China. It was September 8,
feast of Our Lady's nativity, but most of
us were more occupied with the great event
that marked so important a milestone in
Maryknoll's history than with the import of
the feast. Father Price, leader of the mission band, did not enjoy being the center of
attention. He slipped away and went to the
kitchen to give a sister there some final mes-
sages in regard to his Bernadette literature.
The sisters all urged him to go to the re-
fectory, vainly holding out the prospect of a

last opportunity to enjoy Southern fried
chicken, which had been especially prepared
for him. Happily, someone remarked: " But
Father, how can you treat Our Lady so on
her birthday? It's really her party, you
know! "

His eyes opened in childlike wonder.
" Why, that's so! " he exclaimed, and disappeared. And he partook bountifully of
the feast, and never appeared more genial
or more lovable than as Mary's birthday
guest.

From his visit to Lourdes, in 1911, Father
Price brought away a remarkable devotion to
Blessed Bernadette Soubirous, the " Child of
the Immaculate Conception". That he had
some supernatural experience seems quite
certain, although he would never say more
than this: " Something happened to me at
Lourdes. I can never be the same again."
As soon as he returned to America he bent
his energies to making known this favored
child of Mary, and his appeals for the new
work for foreign missions at Maryknoll went

hand in hand with the spread of devotion to
Bernadette and to Mary Immaculate, the
Queen of the Apostles. He had always with
him a number of relics of Bernadette, and
on the third finger of his right hand he wore
what was finally ascertained to be her ring.
He had covered it with black leather, and
naturally it was a never-failing source of
wonder and questioning. When asked what
it was, Father Price used to say: " Well,
now, can you keep a secret? "

On being assured of that, he would smil-
ingly remark, " So can I! " — and there
was an end of it.

His room at Maryknoll was literally filled
with pictures of Bernadette, from large por-
traits on the walls to small prints on his desk
and shelves. On returning from one of his
propaganda trips he was overjoyed to find a
beautiful little imitation of the Lourdes
Grotto set up in one corner of his room —
the work of some Maryknoll confrères.
The beatification of Bernadette gave him
special joy and he celebrated the event by

having a number of medals designed and struck in her honor. The last of these, made just before he left for China, represented the Blessed Virgin appearing to Bernadette at Lourdes and telling her to " pray and work for conversions." Around the rim are the words: " The Message of the Immaculate Conception to every Catholic." On the obverse is the image of Our Divine Redeemer commissioning the Apostles to, " Go, teach all nations "; and the encircling motto is: " All nations to Jesus through The Immaculate Conception."

Father Price also established the Bureau of the Immaculate Conception, to promote devotion to the Blessed Virgin under this title: and he had planned to start a magazine for this purpose when his approaching departure for China made it inadvisable. He prepared in English the only authentic Life of Bernadette of Lourdes, and produced several editions over the name of *J. H. Gregory*. A smaller life of Bernadette, *The Lily of Mary*, also came from his pen. It goes without saying that these books sold at cost, for they were primarily intended to spread devotion to Bernadette and to The Immaculate Conception. They met with a warm welcome and received high praise from the press.

Much more might be added to the delineation of Father Price's saintly character. We might enlarge upon his virtues, his zeal, his extraordinary devotion to Mary Immaculate. But this glimpse into the mind and soul of the man of God will perhaps reveal sufficiently that rare union of the real contemplative with the truly active, which was so strongly marked in him. We are tempted to say that in a contemplative life Father Price would have been supremely happy. And yet, the fruit of his heavenly intercourse was an ever-increasing thirst for souls, to be won through his own tireless activity.

The most striking manifestation of his apostolic zeal came when Father Price at the age of fifty-eight asked to be assigned with the first mission band to leave Maryknoll for the Orient. If we consider that, in addition to the obstacles imposed by age, such a step meant a complete change of life; that it implied the obligation of learning a difficult language; and that it called for constant residence in an enervating climate with a prolonged rainy season that was almost certain to bring on attacks of rheumatism, — we have some comprehension of his yearning for the salvation of immortal souls and of his forgetfulness of self. The first band of missioners was made up, with the exception of Father Price, of inexperienced men but recently ordained, and he rightly felt that his long experience of thirty-three years in the priesthood would be of value in the pioneer days of the China mission. He became the counselor, consoler, model, and inspiration of his three companions, who loved him as a father, and who today, in the midst of their labors, cherish the remembrance of his Christ-like charity and hold his memory in benediction.

Was it a huge mistake for such a man as

Father Price to leave a sphere of certain use-
fulness at home for an uncertain work in the
distant mission fields of the Orient? Some
say that it was. But "the Spirit breathes
where it will," and to follow its call can
never be a mistake. One has only to make
sure, as far as that is possible, that the sum-
mons is from God and not a temptation in
disguise. Father Price acted judiciously,
and gave the question of leaving his life's
work for a new apostolate careful considera-
tion, submitting it to the judgment of holy
and venerable advisers.

His new ministry was a short one — yet
we know that he "lived a long space in a
short time." He left no interpretation of
his life's work with us: not a word came out
of the silence to show what he himself
thought of it, with its light and shade, as he
lay dying so far away from his own Sunny
South. But what an inspiration, to find the
veteran missioner dying in a foreign and
more fruitful field, after a life of untold and
often fruitless labor in his native state!

*MARYKNOLL MISSIONERS AT THEIR
ELDER BROTHER'S GRAVE, HAPPY
VALLEY CEMETERY, HONGKONG*

Many would have yearned for rest and retirement after such a career: one apostolate is usually sufficient for even the most pious and energetic. But Father Price was in the spring of life at fifty-nine years of age, ready to encounter hardships fit to overwhelm the youngest and most fervent levite. Like the Apostle, he always looked on himself as the unprofitable servant and feared to go before God with empty hands. Martyrdom was his desired goal, and the subject of years of prayer. He found it, not as he sought it, but in the mysterious way designed by Providence. Death itself had no power to distress him, save in the thought of pagan souls untaught, and when it came to him in a foreign land it found him ready to go " home ", there to continue his apostolate through the Communion of Saints.

OTHER MARYKNOLL PUBLICATIONS

Maryknoll-At-Ten
A pamphlet history of the Catholic Foreign Mission Society of America.

Field Afar Stories, Vol. I

Field Afar Stories, Vol. II

Field Afar Stories, Vol. III
Separate collections of tales bearing on foreign missions and the foreign-mission vocation.

An American Missionary
Fr. Judge, S.J., in Alaska.

A Modern Martyr
Life and letters of Bl. Theophane Venard.

For the Faith
Just de Bretenières, martyred in Korea in 1866.

The Martyr of Futuna
Bl. Peter Chanel, S.M., martyred in Oceania in 1839.

In The Homes of Martyrs
Visits to the homes and home folk of five young missionary martyrs of the past century.

Observations in the Orient
A survey of Catholic Missions in the Far East — chiefly China and Japan.

The Field Afar
Monthly magazine of the Catholic Foreign Mission Society.

The Maryknoll Junior
Monthly for boys and girls.

For further information, address

THE CATHOLIC FOREIGN MISSION SOCIETY
OF AMERICA
MARYKNOLL : : : NEW YORK